Disclaimer

All information, ideas and guidelines presented here are for educational purposes only. The information presented in this eBook cannot be used as professional financial advice. It does not take your individual state of affairs into consideration so you should look for expert financial advice when needed.

While all possible attempts have been made by the author to verify information provided in this eBook, neither the author nor the publisher will bear responsibility for errors or omissions contained herein.

What's Coming Up Next?

The mortgage process can be really confusing as it has its own vocabulary. There is a lot of paperwork involved and you don't even know what exactly is happening around you. It's just that loans have so many people coming together during the transaction process that the entire task looks extremely complicated. If you don't want to fall for a misleading tactic when it comes to mortgages, you've come to the right place.

Mortgages for the Rest of US unveils complete information about mortgages so that you can decide what will work for you. Continue reading to improve your chances of selecting, signing and closing a dream agreement.

Chapter One: What do Mortgages Really Mean?

You've got to look at a lot of things when you are buying a home than just selecting one that you love. Knowing what you will face during the buying process can save you from a lot of trouble and you can move in easily.

A mortgage, in simple words, is a type of **loan** in which your home acts as the **collateral**. Basically, your mortgage **lender** or the bank gives you "loads" of money to buy a home, which you must repay over a set period of time. This repayment process also involves **interest** and if you are unable to repay the amount, the lending authority can take your home back. This process is also called **foreclosure**.

Wait a minute. We have just started our discussion on mortgages and you have already come across so many complex terms. But, there is nothing to worry about, the only reason this publication has been written is to help you understand the secrets of handling mortgages.

Typically, most books and articles written on this subject are stuffed with confusing industry jargon that only makes your life difficult. This publication on the other hand will actually make mortgages sound easy and a lot different to how mysterious and complicated it looks in real.

You can also find a glossary at the end of this eBook to see a list of terms commonly used in the mortgage industry. Do check out the words highlighted in bold to know more about what they mean.

While reading through the eBook, you can learn about what type of loan you should get, what are the important factors you need to keep in mind before selecting a loan, how you can make your decision more valuable and whether applying for a mortgage is the right choice for you.

Buying a home can be a brain baffling experience for many buyers as they are not very confident when it comes to how much mortgage they really need.

What's really interesting is the fact that mortgage lending has been around for a long time. Things have improved over the years, but there are a few considerations that still make mortgages look nothing less than monsters.

If you've always rented a home, you know what happens when you rent, the story is really simple. You can pack your bags and walk away if your lease agreement is not your type. But you'll understand the problems only when you buy a home and discover things that are not going your way.

There's no landlord to bother you in your dream home, but even then you're the one who has to look into everything and deal with the hassles of ownership. Forget about repairs and other maintenance costs, you have to first do your homework and decide your mortgage payments.

Well, some of you may be thinking "is it really important to apply for a mortgage?" Buying a home can be your dream and looking at the present scenario, you don't have to worry about mortgages only if you have enough cash to buy your home in 'one' payment.

This is highly unlikely and it is better to explore the options you have regarding loans specifically designed to help you buy a home; something we all know as mortgage. You will be surprised to know that before 1930, there was no such thing as a 'loan for buying a home' in the U.S.

Now let's come back to our main discussion. A mortgage is a legal agreement signed between you and the lender.

You will be given a fixed amount of money as a loan, and in most cases; a mortgage is the biggest loan you'll ever borrow. Since you get lots of money in response to your loan application, your home shall act as the collateral.

If you cannot pay back the money to the lender, your home can be taken away and this is surely something you don't want to see. Banks have been the traditional mortgage lenders, and before your application is approved, the bank will look at your income, credit history, saving accounts and bank records to see whether or not you are worthy to get the loan.

Like any other loan, mortgages too have interest rates and need to be repaid within a set period of time. This time frame can range anywhere from five years to thirty years depending on the option you choose.

Mortgages are not only available through banks. Various government agencies and credit unions also offer mortgages and you can shop around to look for the best deal.

What's even more surprising is the fact that insurance companies actually proposed mortgages and not banks, which most of you would assume.

Mortgages came into existence in the early 1930s and it's really no surprise that more than 90% of people were renters before mortgages became common.

The **Federal Housing Administration** (FHA) played a crucial role in setting mortgage requirements thus creating many fruitful opportunities for people like you who want to own their home.

FHA extensively worked on loan qualifications and loan terms to improve your chances of getting approved for a loan. Traditional mortgages were offered for five to seven years and later FHA eventually stretched the period to 30 years.

Different Parts of a Mortgage Payment

You are asked to make a **down payment** on the mortgage before you actually borrow money. You can put as much amount of money as you can in the form of your down payment, and the traditional amount is putting up 20% of the total **purchasing price** of your home.

Remember, the more money you put as down payment, the lower will be the amount you have to borrow.

A typical mortgage payment has the following parts.

- **Principal**

This is the total amount of money you will borrow from a bank or lender after making the down payment.

- **Interest**

This is the amount of money your lender charges you for the loan. Normally, interest is expressed as a percentage of the total amount of money you borrow from the lender.

Interest or additional payment made in the form of interest actually is the "compensation" offered to the lender against a "risk" of loss of principal, which is also known as "**credit risk**".

Credit risk basically is a possibility that you, 'the borrower' may fail to repay the actual amount of loan or principal in the specified time period.

Another reason why lending authorities charge interest is because they need to “forego” or give up other investments, which can prove to be more fruitful only because of you.

Interest in this case is the **opportunity cost**, i.e. the cost of giving up the next best choice, which has to be paid by the borrower, which is you.

A large number of loans given by banks or other lending institutions have total payments distributed or broken down into monthly installments.

For example, if you take a loan, i.e. borrow money from a bank, you will be given a schedule of monthly payments you need to make.

One part of your payment goes in repaying the principal (actual amount of the loan) while the remaining makes up the interest you are supposed to pay.

If you are considered to be a "**low risk**" borrower, you may be charged with a lower interest rate by the lending authority, but if you belong to the "**high risk**" category, you may be charged higher rates for the same amount (principal).

More detail on Mortgage and Interest Rates is coming up in Chapter Six – Mortgage Fundamentals.

If you analyze your monthly payments closely, you will be surprised to know that a significant amount of money you pay to the lender every month only covers the interest due on your amount.

Here's some friendly advice; making minimum loan payments every month will only add to your troubles. This means your principal amount is not reducing at a rate you want it to.

But there is nothing to worry about. Mortgages can become a “win win” situation for you if you make your monthly payments on time. And this publication is here to tell you more about the finer aspects of mortgages.

You can also try paying a little extra money as your monthly payment. This is because the excess amount you pay to the lending authority acts directly on the principal and reduces the total amount of money you owe.

As it is really easy to fall into mortgage traps, let’s briefly see what else you can do to stay safe. Along with making extra payments every month, you should see that you do not add any unnecessary debt, i.e. apply for new loans or credit cards.

You can also try to negotiate with your lending authority and have your interest rate redefined (this is possible only in some cases such as mortgages that don't have fixed interest rates).

Remember, you can be trapped under debt if you don't make the right moves. When you borrow money, you become part of a cycle where every month you need to make a payment which goes into the lender's pocket. The longer you delay the payment, the deeper you get into trouble.

If you are unable to make payments on time, you will be trapped under debt which can prove to be quite harmful for your home. Your interest rates may climb up and require you to pay heavy amounts.

This will slow down the real progress you make measuring the total amount of your debt. You can also lose your home if the same situation continues for a long period of time.

- **Taxes**

Money required to pay your property taxes is put into an **escrow account** that holds property taxes until they are due.

- **Insurance**

Lastly, most mortgages require you to purchase insurance to protect against damages from flood, fire, storm, theft and other calamities. Lenders are not very keen to close the deal if you don't have home insurance which covers your personal property and your home as well.

You need to buy home insurance so that you can afford to repair or rebuild your home in case of accidents. You may buy the coverage for floods even if you don't live in a high risk zone. Mortgages offered by lenders generally are of two types, fixed rate mortgages and adjustable rate mortgages.

Understanding How Much You Have to Pay

Calculation of interest and the amount you have to pay perhaps is one of the most confusing things about mortgages. It's never easy to figure out the payments due on a 30 year fixed rate mortgage at 6% and then suddenly consider a 15 year, fixed rate mortgage at 7% as your second option.

You would come across a term known as **APR** or Annual Percentage Rate. APR is frequently used in mortgage calculation and it is not the same as interest rate. You will find a discussion on things you need to take into account when applying for mortgage later in this eBook. So, how do you know if it's better to go for a mortgage or not at this point in time?

The answer is simple. Continue reading to find out information you need to move ahead in the right direction. The next chapter will tell you how you can analyze your monthly payments, savings, expenses, financial goals and credit ratings to qualify for a loan.

At the end of the next chapter, you will be in a better position to understand how much mortgage you can really afford.

Before heading to the next chapter, let's recall all what we've discussed until now.

- *Mortgages are type of loans that are specifically designed to help you buy a home.*

- *When you take a loan, you sign an agreement with the lender and promise to pay back the amount over the agreed period of time.*
- *Mortgage payments are broadly divided into 4 main categories namely principal, interest, taxes and insurance.*
- *You'll have to pay an extra amount on your loan which is known as Interest. The rate is decided depending on whether you are a high risk borrower or a low risk borrower.*
- *If you cannot repay your loan, the lender has the right to take away your home and recover the amount of money you've borrowed.*

Chapter Two: Discover Your Borrowing Power

You know that you want to buy a new home in a lively town, but there are a lot of decisions you need to make. Things would be even tougher if you've picked a home but don't have a clue of what to do next. You plan to move to that house really soon after getting approved for a mortgage, but will this loan work great for you?

Sometimes just planning things beforehand doesn't really help unless you know whether or not it is the right move. Putting it in simple words, don't just jump into home ownership without determining your borrowing power. This chapter is particularly helpful for those of you who are buying a home for the first time and don't know what size mortgage best suit your needs.

Honestly, you are the only person who can determine your financial situation. If you go to any lender, you will be asked question related to your monthly income, savings, credit history and down payments, but don't assume that the lender knows how you will repay your debt.

For example, have you ever thought about your saving plans or financial situation after retirement? Have you calculated the amount of money you need to spend on your new home or have you decided how you will pay your grocery bills? There are a lot of questions that need to be answered before you actually apply for a mortgage.

Scrutinize Your Monthly Spending

Unless you have someone to fund you, it is important that you save money to buy a new home. Remember, if you have trouble saving money before buying a home, you need to a keep eye on your savings after you make the purchase.

Because you, or in fact no one, has a clue about what will happen in the near future, you have to first assess your monthly income and spending to decide how much you can save. After you decide the amount you can save easily, you can go ahead and figure out the amount you can borrow.

Even though it sounds challenging, trying to save is not a difficult thing to do. All you have to do at this point in time is work through your monthly budget and determine whether or not you can squeeze out $2000 to $4000 every month as your mortgage payment.

Determining the exact size of mortgage at this point is not important and even rough estimates are enough. It would be wise to design a saving schedule only after you've put everything in the right place. Here's a friendly piece of advice; buy a home only if you can afford it, not just because someone told you that you can make lots of money in real estate.

Find out Your Credit Rating

Unless you have money stuffed inside your pillows, you need a good **credit rating** to get the best mortgage options. Without a good credit history, you'll find yourself under attack by high interest rates, bigger fees and fewer mortgage options in the worst case.

Why shouldn't you take a chance? Remember, poor credit rating can actually reduce your chances of qualifying for a loan and you can never buy your dream home.

Regardless of the loan plan you choose, your lender pulls out your credit report to determine whether or not you have the ability to repay the mortgage.

In most cases, your credit history is judged by the numbers generated by the credit bureaus, which are also known as "FICO scores." Tips to raise your **FICO score** effectively are coming up in Chapter Three and Four.

The major credit bureaus collect data about your history of borrowing and put them together in your credit report. You can expect your lender to accept your application and offer you lower interest rates and more importantly, more loan choices when your score ranges between 760 and 850.

If your score is 620 or lower, you will be placed in the "subprime" category, and you might be asked to pay significantly higher interest rates for your loan. It is possible that you get fewer options to choose from. Generally, a FICO score of about 500-520 is what is required to qualify you for a mortgage.

Of course, credit score is not only what you need to focus on. It is important that you scrutinize your credit report from time to time and make sure that your entries are correct. Remember, mistakes on your credit report can lower your scores and affect you badly.

Pick Your Own Financial Goals

The other factor that controls the amount of money you can borrow is your own set of personal financial goals.

After reading through the first few pages, you know that applying for a mortgage perhaps is the biggest financial decision of your life. Before you get a mortgage, make sure that your loan application does not conflict with your short-term and long-term goals.

Remember, tracking your personal goals closely is the key to achieving your next target, i.e. your dream home. Before you start working on the amount you have to borrow, make a list of your personal goals and arrange them in order of importance.

Regardless of your age, you are likely to have some sort of short and long-term goals in mind. Prioritizing your goals is the first step and your financial goals can be as extensive as you want. You may be very young and retirement seems years away, but even then, determine a rough amount you'll need to spend the rest of your life peacefully.

Similarly, figure out how much money you'll need to achieve other goals and don't worry even if the amount is overwhelming. Sometimes, you need to change your saving and spending habits in order to 'free' money that can be used to buy a home.

Use your initial list to see all areas you can cut down expenses and save more money. If you feel confident that you can generate the amount for your monthly payment, there is no harm in going ahead with your plan.

Determine How Much You Can Afford

In addition to your personal finances and credit history, there is one important thing you need to figure out before applying for a home loan. This shouldn't be difficult to guess. You have to determine how much you can afford and how much your lender will allow you to borrow.

To determine your affordability, you have to first determine your gross monthly income. Make sure you include all sources of regular and recurring income in the list. Don't forget to include assets such as real estate and stocks and use them in the calculation. If you have a question about any specific asset or source of income, you can always refer to a good loan officer.

After you finalize your monthly income, it is time to move towards your monthly debt. List all your monthly obligations on a sheet of paper, for example, your credit cards, auto finance loans, other personal loans and ongoing obligations such as child support. If you use a credit card, stick to minimum monthly credit card payment during the calculation process.

You can of course, control your credit use and free more money for making your mortgage payments. And, you can also rule out the debts that will be paid off in the next six months. In the end, add up all the debts to determine your monthly debt amount.

Well, you shouldn't be surprised if your application is rejected only because your debts were on a higher side. Most lenders don't really want to deal with clients that have a doubtful ability to repay. Even though every bank and lender has a slightly different formula for approving applications, here's what they normally look at.

- **Your Monthly Expense**

Your monthly expenses should not exceed 28% of your monthly income. You should also consider monthly payments for taxes and insurance when you calculate your expenses. If you don't have a clear idea, you can estimate that 15 percent of your income can go towards this expense.

- **Your Monthly Expense And Your Total Monthly Debt Combined**

Both the factors in combination cannot exceed 36% of your gross monthly income if you want your application to be approved.

Depending on your individual situation, you can be given flexibility in the 28% and 36% guidelines. Lenders might consider your application if you are borrowing less than 80% of the total value of your home. This is likely if you are making a large cash down payment.

Likewise, you don't really need to worry about your income and expenses if a rich friend or family member is willing to **cosign** on the agreement with you. Even your lender will be less strict on the guidelines if you have someone to cosign the loan with you.

Remember that you have many options when it comes to mortgages and each option has a different set of rules. So don't be discouraged if you cannot afford a lot of money in one go. You might choose to apply for an adjustable rate mortgage to keep your dream home within reach. Meanwhile, you can work hard to save more money and keep your monthly payments under check.

It's now time to recall all what've discussed in this chapter.

- *Determining your monthly spending is half the battle on your way to getting the best mortgage.*
- *After you examine your spending and income, take out time to figure out how little you are saving. Remember, good saving skills can really come in handy when you have to squeeze out money for your monthly mortgage payment.*
- *Don't neglect your credit rating when you decide to buy a new home. If you are planning to apply for a mortgage, make sure your FICO score is more than 520.*
- *Most people find it convenient to use their monthly income and monthly debt load to*

determine the size of mortgage they can afford. You also increase your chances of getting qualified for the loan if your monthly expenses and debt do not exceed 36% of your gross monthly income.

Chapter Three: Will Your Application Be Selected?

Getting approved for a mortgage depends on a lot on what your lender thinks. If your lender feels that you can afford this particular debt, that's all you need to get a mortgage. You must be willing to make your payments on time, and remember, it is really hard to get out of the debt trap if you plunge deep inside.

Know How Lenders Determine Your Fate

Since lenders are giving you lots of money in response to your request, they want to know a lot about you before approving your application. They want to confirm that you will meet their requirements and that their investment is not risky.

There are no definite rules when it comes to questions a lender can ask you. But, most probably questions asked will be related to your income, employment history, debt records, savings, financial assets, purpose of loan, amount of down payment you are willing to make and how you will use your property.

You are not the only one who is applying for a mortgage, so your lender also has to choose the right candidate from a number of applicants. If you meet the criteria set by your lender, your application is more likely to be accepted.

- **Employment History**

If you plan to apply for a mortgage, you'll have to tell the details about your current employer, total amount you make, how long you've been working in the current position and how do you receive your income.

Things may turn in your favor if you have a steady income, but if your income is irregular, you need to provide more details to convince your lender and get a favorable deal.

- **Outstanding Debts**

Your standing debt is another factor that largely determines the way lenders see you. If you have a large number of recurring debts, you need to work harder to impress your lender.

This however does not mean that your application will not be approved. Pull out your auto loan records, credit card history, savings details and other financial records to prove your worthiness as a borrower. It is important that you estimate how much money will be left after you clear your down payment and other associated costs.

- **Down Payment**

Lenders want to hear the amount of money you are putting down as down payment. You may be asked questions in a conversational style and you have to tell where the money will come from.

- **Others**

The lenders don't really ask questions about your credit history, but they are interested to know about your current bank balance. You might have to clarify the purpose of your loan and whether your loan will be used to buy a new home or refinance.

You can expect good results after entering into a negotiation with your lender if:

- You have a steady employment or have a work experience of more than two years in the same profession.

- Your monthly debt and spending is less than 36% of your total monthly income.

- You have no recent large buys such as cars.

- You are putting down 5% of the total sale price of your home as down payment.

- You will be left with money for making at least two mortgage monthly payments in your bank account after closing.

- Your home will be used as your own residence.

On the other hand, the following conditions may work against you.

- Being self employed or having irregular income.
- Total debt-to-income ratio is more than 36%.
- Your credit cards are maxed out.
- The property you intend to buy will be used for leasing.
- Not enough cash is left in your bank account after clearing closing costs.
- You put less than 3% of total sales price as down payment.

What To Do if You Have Poor Credit History

The recent credit crisis has made really difficult for people to get approved for a mortgage. So it's important that you pay close attention to your credit history and work hard to improve your score. Having a good report can be the turning point in locking the best deal with the best interest rates. What should you do if your credit history is not in good shape?

Here are some tips to help you fix minor flaws in your credit report.

- **Do Check Your Credit Report On A Regular Basis**.

When you apply for a mortgage, the first thing your lender looks at is your credit history. Your lender pulls out your credit report and checks for your payment history along with a list of things. More details regarding credit report is coming up in Chapter Four.

Checking your report regularly will let know you whether there is anything that is affecting your rating adversely. You'll never know which credit report will be pulled by your lender, so it is better if you check the reports generated by all three major credit bureaus. You can also get a free online copy of your credit report and do visit the credit bureau official website for more information.

- **Don't forget to correct inaccurate information on your report.**

Here's a piece of friendly advice. Misinformation or inaccuracy on your credit report is as harmful as poor credit scores. Remember, inaccurate information on credit report can get your application rejected. If you spot any inaccurate information, contact the credit bureau immediately.

- **Get rid of delinquent accounts.**

Lenders are not pleased with people who don't make their payments on time. If you have any

delinquent accounts, consider your chances to be very bleak. Make sure you pay off all your accounts before you apply for a mortgage if you really don't want to kill your chances.

- **Change your payment habits.**

Once you establish a schedule for making your payments on time, your life is going to get easier. All you have to do is change your habits and increase your chances of getting approved for a mortgage.

If you spot a recent late payment, clear your dues and wait for at least six months before filing in your mortgage application. Your delinquencies would be older then, and this will make your credit report look a lot better.

- **Work on your debt to income ratio.**

This may sound complicated but you need to reduce your debt to almost 12% of your total monthly income. This not only will favor your credit rating, but you have greater chances of getting approved for a loan. Remember, your debt to income ratio is going to skyrocket when your mortgage is approved so it is better if you prepare for it beforehand.

- **Keep a close eye on your FICO scores**

Your lenders get a clear idea of where your credit stands after looking at the numbers so make sure your numbers are on the higher side. You can know your current scores from myFICO.com.

Generally, a total score of 720 gives you a real good chance to get low interest rates on your loan. If your score is lower, you need to fix your rating. More tips to improve your score are coming up in the next chapter.

- **Stay away from new debt.**

It is a wise move to keep away any new debt from appearing on your credit report until your mortgage application is approved. This will help maintain your credit score on the higher side as your total debt is going to stay below 12% of your total income.

On a separate note, you have to remember that every new credit inquiry affects your credit score. So stay from new debt until you convince your lender about your financial stability and get approved for a mortgage.

Find Out How Much You Can Get

You already know that lenders do not decide a maximum mortgage amount out of thin air when you apply for a loan. The loan amount approved depends on a number of a factors and the total amount you receive from your lender is assumed to be the exact amount you will be able to manage considering your financial standing.

You've got to pay attention to two important factors when looking at the size of your mortgage payment. The first is the size of your loan and the second is the total term of your loan.

Size of your mortgage loan signifies the amount you will receive and 'term' refers to the total length of time you have to repay the full amount.

Here's a quick formula to help you understand things. There is an inverse relationship between the size of your monthly payment and mortgage term.

If you select a mortgage plan with longer term, you'll have to make smaller monthly payments. This is the main reason why most people go for 30 year mortgages.

Do You Know How Lenders Determine Mortgage You Qualify For?

Mortgage lenders have different rules of thumbs or formulae to calculate how much they will lend you. After reading through the initial pages of this eBook, most of you would be familiar with the two most common ratios used by lenders.

Here's a brief description to help you recall what we've discussed earlier.

- Total monthly housing costs in comparison to your total monthly income.

Lenders want to see your mortgage payment to be less than 28% of your total monthly income. You need to inform your lender about the total income you receive every month.

It is better if you deduct your expenses to get a much accurate amount. As mentioned earlier, your total housing costs should not exceed 28% of your total monthly income.

In technical terms, this is called the **Front Ratio**. Lenders assess your gross income from your business records and tax returns.

Basically the lender wants to guarantee that you pay your property taxes because local governments can seize real estate to recover property taxes that remain unpaid.

The government's rights dominate the lender's ownership rights so lenders are more likely to approve applicants who pay property taxes on time.

- Debt to Income ratio.

Your monthly expenses including car loans, credit card payments, installment loans, student loans and other commitments should not exceed 36% of your monthly income.

Obviously, if you have lots of debt and you can only barely make the minimum payments, you're not a good prospect for any lender.

Lenders typically reject applications where total debt payments (including the mortgage payment) exceed 36% of the applicant’s total monthly income. In technical terms, this is known as the **Back Ratio** or **total expense ratio**.

Most lenders focus more on credit history to decide whether your loan will be approved or not. Lenders can make a more informed decision after looking at your credit score, also known as the FICO score. Credit rating also comes in handy if you have applied for a loan preapproval.

The reason lenders pull out your credit report and not any other document is the fact that it represents accurate stats about your financial standing. Every detail about your payment history, outstanding debt and number of accounts is displayed on your report.

It's easier to obtain a loan or get prequalified for a mortgage when you have a higher credit score. On the other hand, if you have the habit of making late payments, your credit report will not be in good shape.

A low score may compel a lender to reject your application or ask you to make a large down payment. It is also likely that lenders propose high interest rates for the loan to reduce the risk they are willing to take on you.

You can analyze your debt to get your records into acceptable ratios. When looking at your credit report, make sure you figure out ways to:

- Pay off any debt and credit balances you easily can. Many lenders are happy to approve borrowers that have removed their monthly obligations within six months.

- Keep track of all accounts under your name. This is important if you have cosigned for a friend or a family member. Do have proper documentation to prove that your friend or family member is making the necessary payments on time.
- Prove that you are likely to earn more in the future. Lenders can stretch your amount if you demonstrate the ability to improve your credit rating in a short period of time or manage higher payments.

Having said all this, you can stick to one rule to make your application more appealing to a lender. Lower your Debt to Income ratio because this is one of the most effective tools to achieve lower interest rate and lower costs.

Also, the lender wants to make sure that your house is insured. Honestly, your lender doesn't want you to walk away from your agreement to repay your loan because your home was flooded or burned up in a fire. You will be asked to provide insurance details before a lender actually grants you money.

Another formula used by lenders to determine the total amount they can give you is the **Loan to Value Ratio.**

This is calculated by dividing your mortgage principal by the current market value of your home. Most lenders want you to put down 10% or 20% of down payment before your application is approved.

The higher the down payment you make, your application has more chances of getting approved. Lenders know that your home is less likely to foreclose since you invested more money. Technically, higher down payment lowers the risk for the lender and helps you seal a deal with lower interest rate.

You will be pleased to know that only 2% of people who put down 20% or more as down payment fail to make the mortgage payments on time.

The Truth About Loan Prequalification

Loan prequalification does not guarantee that you will become a proud owner of your dream home, but it does help your lender know how much you can borrow and what you can pay in terms of a monthly mortgage payment.

Getting prequalified for a loan simply means that you have made a list of your income, savings, assets and monthly expenses and submitted the information to your lender. Usually lenders use this information to decide whether or not your application qualifies their criteria.

Mortgage prequalification is something you would hear when you interact with mortgage lenders. If a mortgage lender prequalifies you, this means that lender is willing to approve your application and extend the loan if all of the information you presented is correct.

To get prequalified, you need to talk to a reputable loan officer and give them details about yourself. On most occasions, prequalification is a simple process and you can even do it over the phone.

The loan officer would ask questions related to your income, employment and credit history. You have to tell how much you earn and how long you have been working with your current employer.

Some of the questions asked by the loan officer would also deal with your credit history and outstanding debt.

Based on the information you provide, the loan officer can give you an approximate figure about the loan you can get. However, you need to understand that the loan officer has not approved your loan.

At this point in time, the lender has not verified any information about your income nor has contacted your employer. At the end of the prequalification process, you will only know how much mortgage you can truly afford.

There is another term known as Mortgage preapproval and preapproval is considered better than prequalification. Most real estate agents and even sellers are keen to interact with buyers that are already preapproved.

Basically, mortgage preapproval shows that you are very serious about buying a home and that the deal can move very quickly after a suitable offer is made.

Therefore, if you really want to make an impression on the lender when buying a home, preapproval will definitely be a good route to take. Wonder how this is possible?

The preapproval process is going to be much more detailed and extensive when compared to a simple mortgage prequalification. You have to fill out an application form and submit specific information about yourself to your lender.

Your lender will need your Social Security number and they will also access your credit history. Preapproval process can take long because your lender will take time to review your credit history and debt record. The lender will also calculate your Debt to Income ratio and contact your current employer to verify the details you have provided.

You might be asked to provide documentation related to tax returns and income details. Once you get preapproved for a loan, you can get the mortgage as soon as you select your dream property.

The next chapter will discuss a few secrets about credit ratings, but before moving forward let's recall all what've discussed until now.

- *Lenders use your credit history, employment details and outstanding debt to decide whether or not you are a good prospect.*
- *Having good credit score improves your chances of being selected.*
- *Lenders accept or reject your application with the help of two common ratios namely front*

ratio and back ratio. Another ratio, Loan to Value ratio is also used.

- *Getting preapproved for a loan is better than getting prequalified. Preapproval process is longer and is considered more reliable. Most real estate agents want to work with people who are preapproved.*

Chapter Four: Insider Secrets You Need to Know About Credit

Now when we are talking about credit, there are quite a few secrets that you need to know. Knowing the secrets really well can help you understand what all is involved in building your credit history and you will not suffer due to poor credit scores.

Let's start off with what exactly is a credit score. Your credit score basically is a numeric value that shows your creditworthiness as a borrower. The numbers usually range from 330 to 850 and the values are derived by a formula put forward by Fair Isaac Company.

Your credit or FICO score helps lenders assess whether or not they should give you money.

How do Lenders Rate Your Creditworthiness?

Lenders normally use your credit report to rate your creditworthiness. Whenever you apply for new credit, the lender pulls out your report and checks the records to know whether or not you are a good prospect.

Since mortgage involves lots of money, lenders may take their own time to verify information your credit report provides to decide your fate.

Finding ways to make sure that your credit report looks perfect is a difficult task, especially if you don't know where to start.

The credit bureaus that evaluate and rate your creditworthiness don't tell you all the rules of the game, therefore, many of you will not know how you should rebound from a poor credit record.

You already know that credit reports are generated by special agencies commonly known as credit bureaus. There are three major national credit bureaus in the United States, namely Experian, TransUnion and Equifax.

You would also find local and regional credit agencies/bureaus. Each credit bureau generates a credit report and lists the following information in different order, but the basic information remains the same.

- **PERSONAL INFORMATION**

This section shows your name, social security number, phone numbers, address, spouse's name and date of birth. You would also find your current and previous phone numbers and addresses listed in this category.

- **ACCOUNT INFORMATION**

Your credit report shows account information as reported by your creditors. Your credit accounts can be classed as "GOOD STANDING" or "DEROGATORY" on the basis of positive and negative feedback provided by your creditors.

You will find creditor's Information including name and contact details. Your account status appears next and classifies your accounts as OPEN, CLOSED, IN COLLECTION, PAID, NEVER LATE, CHARGED OFF etc.

Additional information featured in this section includes date you opened the account, date of last activity, type of account (this includes auto loan, mortgage or credit card), credit limit and maximum balance you owe on the account(s).

One of the reasons lenders choose to pull out your credit report is the fact that it lists your payment history in detail. Not only do lenders get to know the balance you owe on a particular account, but they also know the details of your most recent payments.

Unfortunately, your credit report clearly displays payments you have missed and it also features the number of times you've missed a payment, date missed and how late your payment is (for example, 30, 60, 90 days).

- **CREDIT INQUIRIES**

Your lenders also get a clear idea about your recent credit applications after having a look at your report. Whenever you apply for a new credit card, installment loan or a mortgage, the lenders are authorized to pull out your credit report.

Every credit inquiry against your name is treated as a hard inquiry and it actually reduces your FICO score. So don't be surprised to see low credit scores if you apply for new credit quite often.

Here's a friendly reminder. If you find any unfamiliar credit inquiry on your report, don't waste anymore time and get the record corrected immediately. Remember, false inquiry or information on your report can actually turn the decision against you.

- **PUBLIC REPORT**

The last section of credit report is titled **Public Report.** Here you can find information about overdue child payments, court actions, bankruptcy and liens. Remember, public report listing can show on your credit report for seven to ten years depending upon the type of record.

Lenders determine your creditworthiness after looking at how well you have managed to handle your accounts, credit and finances. The credit score you get in the end is all what matters the most to any lender. If you have a good score, you have many options when it comes to mortgages, and most importantly, you'll get a loan with the best interest rate.

What is a Good Credit Score?

A number of different categories make up your total credit score and here's a brief description to help you understand better.

- **Payment History**

This comprises about 35% of your total credit score and the term is not really difficult to understand. You need to remember one simple rule: Delaying payments damages your score whereas making payment on time will help you increase your score.

- **Total Amount Owed**

This category focuses on the amount of money you owe to your creditors. Make sure you keep a close eye on your home loans, car loans or credit cards to score high in this category. An easy way to boost your credit score is keeping your balances low compared to your total credit limits.

- **Length of Credit History**

This category reviews all of your credit accounts and rates them looking at the opening dates. So if you want to earn more points, keep your old credit accounts in good shape.

- **Types of Credit**

Your credit score is going to be high when you have a mix of different types of accounts. Try to keep a healthy mix of credit card, car loans and mortgage to raise your credit score.

- **New Credit Inquiry**

As mentioned earlier, a new inquiry is listed on your report whenever you apply for new credit. A large number of inquiries on your credit report indicates that you are actively seeking credit and this may work against you. To keep your credit rating safe and score high in this category, apply for new credit only when you really need it.

FICO scores

FICO scores are the most common type of credit scores used today. The scores are updated on a monthly basis and range from 300 to 850. Your

FICO score changes when your creditors report your performance to a credit bureau.

Remember, lenders are really impressed by high FICO scores and you have better chances of getting a mortgage when your report shows numbers on the higher side. On the other hand, the lower your score, the harder it is for you to convince your lenders and get a mortgage.

Most lenders will not feel confident to lend you money and it is likely that you are charged higher interest rates. To get the best mortgage deals, your score should be 720 or higher. Here's a chart to help you understand how FICO scores are rated.

FICO credit scores range from 330 to 830

- Scores over **720** are considered to be **EXCELLENT**
- Scores of **680 to 720** are **GOOD**

- Scores of **620 To 680** are considered **FAIR**
- Scores below **620** are **BAD** and
- Scores below **580** are **VERY POOR**

In addition to making late payments, your credit scores are damaged by unemployment, unexpected high expenses such as medical emergency or divorce and bankruptcy.

Know Some Innovative Ways to Fix Poor Credit

Wonder what are the steps you can take to speed up your credit repair? Of course, repairing or fixing credit is not impossible; however, you need to understand that it takes time.

There are no magic quick fixes, but here are a few tips you can use to erase your bad credit record. In the end, you will be quite pleased with your effort, especially if you have been under a great deal of stress due to bad credit or outstanding debt.

Your credit report displays your credit record and helps lenders determine your creditworthiness. You can use your credit report to determine areas you need to work on and improve your credit score. But before we discuss ways you can fix poor credit, let's see all what is not included in your credit report.

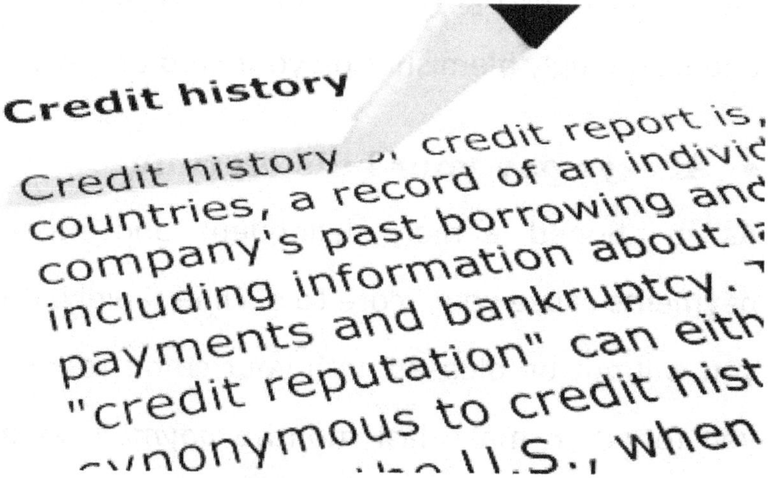

Information about saving accounts, bankruptcies that are more than 10 years old and debts that have been charged off are never featured under any section of your report. Moreover, your credit report gives no clue about your religion, political views, past medical history or criminal records.

If you have been suffering from poor credit, you can try doing the following to give a positive boost to your score. Remember, this is going to take some time so it is important that you stick to your good habits. Even the smallest good habits will get you going in the right direction, so let's get started and fix the ugly blemishes on your credit report.

- **Always pay your bills on time.**

As mentioned earlier, delinquent and missed payments cause your score to decline rapidly. And you will not be pleased with your credit report if you forget to make last month's *payment* **every month**!

If you have problems remembering the important dates, you've got plenty of tools such as calendars, Outlook reminders and to-do-lists to help you with the task.

- **In case you miss a payment, work hard to get current and try to stay current.**

Because missed payments damage your credit scores in the long run, it is important that you settle your debt and try to keep pace with your payment schedule.

Unfortunately, the credit bureau counts you as a careless borrower even if you have been over 90 days late just once in your life. You will be surprised to know that a single 90 day late payment damages your credit score the same way bankruptcy or a tax lien does.

If you continue to miss your payments beyond 30 or 60 days, you show that you are more likely to miss your future payments and this will damage your score in the long run. Now that you know how badly your credit score will suffer due to your habits, your foremost goal should be to make payments on time.

- **Dust off your debt completely rather than hiding them under a carpet!**

Now this is something you need to understand clearly. Before you decide to fool your lender by shifting your debt to other accounts, know that this will not make you a good customer.

Pay off your debt completely even if this does not remove the blemishes instantly. Remember, clearing off debt completely won't rebuild your credit score immediately, but if you continue to manage your debt and make payments on time, your credit report will definitely improve over time.

- **Apply for new credit and open credit accounts only if you need them.**

In case you open a new account, manage them responsibly and make your payments on time.

- **Keep a close eye on your credit limits.**

Managing credit cards effectively over a long period of time can have a positive impact on your credit score. Remember, lenders want to see a huge gap between your credit limit and the amount you are using. Try to keep your balances low on credit cards and use your card 'lightly.'

You often can improve your scores by limiting your card usage to 30% or even less of what is allowed as your card's limit. It is excellent if you try to restrict your card usage to 10% of the total card limit.

If you're having trouble making ends meet, contact your credit card companies to help set up email or text alerts. You'll be notified when you're close to crossing the limit you've set for yourself.

You don't need to worry even if you have a really bad credit score at the moment. Your credit score is not permanent and improves when you add positive information to your credit report over time. Repairing your credit history by using your credit card responsibly and making payments on time will raise your FICO score gradually, so it is important that check your credit report on a regular basis to know your progress.

Your Credit Report Can Make a Big Difference in Fixing Your Credit History

If you really want to improve your credit score, it is important that you know where you stand now. Maybe your credit score is OK, but your credit report isn't. Are you still confused?

Often your credit score drops only because your credit report features missing or false information. But there is nothing to worry about. You can save yourself from trouble by checking your report for errors. It is true that a single piece of information does not determine the fate of your mortgage application, but it is always better to keep your records accurate and up to date.

A creditor or lender also looks at other information such as your monthly income, nature of employment, and the amount of loan you have applied for. After looking at your credit history and the information you've provided, a lender may approve you for a loan even with a low score or reject your application even if you have a good score. However, if you get approved with a low credit score, you'll have to pay higher interest rates

If you notice any discrepancy on your report, waste no more time and contact the credit bureau(s) immediately. You can also review your credit report online by visiting www.annualcreditreport.com

Managing Your Credit History

Just when you feel like you are making good progress, it is time you push yourself harder. Apparently, your credit scores will improve when you change your habits and this is nothing less than a great achievement. Don't panic if the result is not what you had expected.

Sometimes, 'plateaus' are extremely frustrating especially if you don't notice any signs of improvement over a long period of time. After recovering from your bad credit habits, you need to keep the following three things in mind to keep moving in the right direction.

1. Identify and learn from your mistakes.
2. Focus on fixing your credit report so that no more blemishes are left on it.
3. Continue building your creditworthiness and maintain great scores.

The report generated when you log on to www.myfico.com gives you a good idea about your current financial standing. For example:

- You find your FICO score in bold number right at the top.
- The illustration also shows your score relates to other consumers based in the U.S.

- You also get a clear picture about how your report looks to a potential lender.

As mentioned earlier, **FICO scores range from 300-850** and you must try to keep the numbers on a higher side. By taking a look at your credit report, you've already taken the first step to manage your credit history. Wonder how does your online FICO report look like? Here is a sample figure to give a better idea.

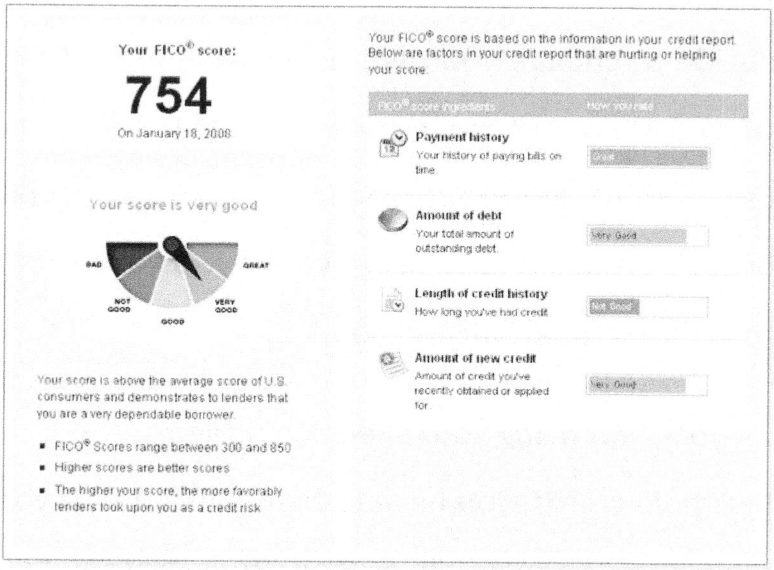

Image Source: http://www.myfico.com/

See, it's just so easy to make your plans after looking at this report because you know the areas you need to work on. Your next step should be to find out ways you can improve your credit and manage your performance.

Here are a few steps that guarantee credit success.

1. Know your starting point.

Imagine that you want to get into shape and decide to change your diet. How do you go about it? You start with your current weight, right? Try using the same approach to manage credit history. You already know your FICO score and this is your ideal starting point.

2. Focus on fixing your specific problems.

In simple words, you have to be credit smart if you really want to maintain a good credit history. You won't notice much success if you try to improve your credit blindly. Of course, you don't have to be a credit expert to understand the do's and don'ts of managing credit. Make sure you focus on areas you feel require more work and check whether or not your plan is working.

3. Do some research about what really builds and destroys your credit score.

After you've become familiar with areas that need some work, you can really attack your problems from the core when you become more knowledgeable about credit.

For example: Take a closer look at factors that make up your credit score. After reading through the last few pages, you know that your payment history is one of the most important factors that determine your FICO score. Your credit score also depends on the length of your credit history and the number of new credit inquiries.

So, you can deal with your credit problems more effectively when you stay current with your report and understand how you need to deal with problems.

4. Check your report regularly.

You will be surprised to know that most people check their credit report only when they have to make a major purchase. Unfortunately, not many problems can be corrected at the last minute and this leaves you with limited options when it comes to getting the best loan.

You need to check your credit score every couple of months especially if you've outlined an improvement plan. You have to know whether your plan is working, right? Experts recommend that you must check your credit twice a year and at least 6 months before applying for a loan or making a major purchase.

5. Never ignore the mistakes on your credit report.

If your credit report contains errors, you need to make sure that the mistakes are corrected as soon as possible. You can find mistakes in your report if:

- You applied for credit using different names

- Someone made an error while entering your name or personal information
- Your social security number is misread by the lender
- Your payments are reported to the wrong account

What Should You Do If You Spot Mistakes In Your Report?

Both the credit bureau and company that provided the information are responsible for correcting inaccurate or false information under the Fair Credit Reporting Act.

First, inform the credit bureau in writing about the information you feel is incorrect and include copies of documents that support your say. You have to provide your complete name and address to the credit bureau and request correction of information.

In addition, you also have to inform the appropriate creditor or authority that you are disputing the information they have provided to the bureau.

This chapter should clear all the doubts you had about credit. Knowing the basics of what makes up your FICO score can help you manage your credit history in a better way and you can improve your chances of signing the best mortgage deal.

As always, let us recall the 'credit secrets' we've learned so far.

- *Your credit or FICO score is not the only factor that determines whether or not you can get a mortgage. Your lender will look at other information such as; amount of debt you can handle, your employment history, credit history and monthly income, to decide the amount of credit you can get.*

- *Your credit score is just a "snapshot" of your credit performance at a particular point in time. This score changes gradually and you can actually improve your score by dealing with your credit problems. Your score will slowly move to the higher side when you continue to add new positive information to your report as time passes.*

- *Making a plan to improve your credit score can help you bag a more favorable deal. Don't forget to check out Chapter Six to know how improved scores can lower mortgage interest rates.*

Chapter Five: Easy Steps for Locating the Best Loan

Buying a home is an important step and most buyers struggle to make ends meet. Even you would be confused and it's never easy to keep track of the varying interest rates and terms different lenders offer.

Having said this, it is not impossible to find a loan that suits your requirements. All you have to do is take out time and do some research. The first step in selecting the best loan is choosing a lender. Let us first see the tricks that'll help you find the best lender in the industry.

How Should You Select a Lender?

As mentioned earlier, if you're buying a home, you'll need a mortgage. And before you get the money, you'll have to know the different mortgage lenders who are willing to help you with the process.

You can make a choice by browsing through the list of mortgage providers available online. If you are not very keen to use the internet, you can check your local newspapers and directory to know some of the most competitive mortgage lenders in your own area.

The local newspaper you receive daily is one of the best places to check out local mortgage lenders. You'll also come across some of the best deals and quotes available in your region. It is always better to work with a reputable local lender because both of you will be more familiar with the local demographics.

Moreover, lots of paperwork also needs to be pulled together during the loan-acquisition process. When working with a local lender, you can easily keep track of your progress, something that takes more time and effort if you have to deal with an online lender.

This, however, does not mean you stop searching for lenders online. Make sure that the online lender you select keeps you updated about the process and you'll be good to go.

Asking your friends and colleagues for recommendations is also helpful. Since you don't know all the details, ask friends and colleagues who have recently made purchases. Once you pick a lender of your choice, don't forget to ask the following questions to make a final decision.

1. What interest rate do you consider to offer me?
2. Does your loan have any additional fee or payment?

   If the lender refuses to answer this, it is not wise to do further business. Go find another lender who answers all your questions.
3. Can you give me an estimate featuring all my costs and fee?
4. Will the interest rate fluctuate or stay locked? If I lock-in the interest rate on my loan, how much will it cost?
5. How much down payment is required for my loan?

   Generally, mortgages require a 20% down payment, but your lender can tell you more about the options you have when you reveal how much of a down payment you can make.

6. How can I get a mortgage prequalification or preapproval letter?
7. Is there a prepayment penalty on my loan?

You don't have to obtain a mortgage that has a prepayment penalty. If your lender is offering you a loan with penalty, maybe this choice isn't the best you can get. Continue searching for other options until you find a better deal.

There are a number of different fees lenders charge you in connection with your loan. Interestingly, different lenders can have different names for them. So, if you are looking for the best lender, you should look at the total fee they are going to charge you.

Generally, the lender can ask you to pay money as processing fee, mortgage insurance premium, appraisal fee, the cost of your credit report, application fee, commitment charges and wire transfer fee.

Can You Go with a Mortgage Broker?

Another important question you need to answer is whether you should go searching for a mortgage on your own or use a mortgage broker. Interestingly, mortgage brokers claim to help you locate the best deal among several lenders. However, you have to be careful and weigh the strengths and weaknesses of a broker before working with an agent of your choice.

Simply put, a good mortgage broker can help you do some research and find the best lender. What you don't really know at this point is the fact that a mortgage broker is not obligated to find the deal that best fits your needs. Yes, mortgage brokers can encourage you to go for deals that offer the brokers more profits instead of favoring you.

So, it is better if you talk with a couple of your potential broker's clients to know how the experience was. If they received good deals and the closing was smooth, you can go ahead and hire the same mortgage broker. Make sure the broker helps you find the deals that are in line with your expectations.

Here's a friendly reminder. Even if you decide to work with a mortgage broker, do spend some time researching about other lenders. This should help you judge whether the deal your broker comes up with is rightly the best deal for you.

Selecting the Best Plan – Know What Will Work for You

You are aware of the fact that comparing loans from different lenders is one of the most difficult parts of mortgage shopping. Your task becomes even more complicated when you have to handle a lot of things besides interest rates.

Firstly, you have to understand that mortgages consist of **quoted rate, points** and other factors such as **closing costs**. Most mortgage lenders allow you to pick your own combination of rate and points for a loan, therefore, don't forget to compare the associated points when choosing a particular product.

When you are comparing lenders, it is important that you compare "loan related fee" lenders charge to approve your loan. This is because other costs are not directly related to the lender, hence; don't make much of a difference. Secondly, you also have to investigate and compare all loan features before making a final decision. More details about loan features are coming up in Chapter Seven.

Another thing you need to consider when comparing different loans is the **lock-in period.** Generally, lock-ins of 30, 45 or 60 days are quite common. Interestingly, the price of your loan increases with an increase in the lock-in period. Therefore, lock-in period you select should be long enough for the settlement of your loan.

Here's something you need to remember. If you are comparing loans based on the interest rates they offer, make sure you compare them on the same day. This is because interest rates change daily and you may not get a clear idea if you compare two products on two different days.

Second, you should only compare different loans of the same type. Actually, it is senseless to compare different products otherwise you will be comparing apples and oranges. For example, comparing a 30-year fixed mortgage with 15-year adjustable mortgage makes no sense.

Surfing the Web

You will be pleased to know that the internet is also a good choice for comparing different mortgage products. You can browse through different websites and select a product that offers the lowest interest rates. You may find the best deal on the internet, but there are a number of hidden facts.

Sometimes, you may be surprised by higher interest rates or hidden costs when you contact the lender. This is because not all websites and online deals are reliable and it is very important to pick up a product that is secure. You can decide on a type of product you would like to have and then search for reputable lenders that offer the same.

As mentioned earlier, you should compare similar products if you don't want your comparison to get into a complete mess. To make sure things get done the right way, write down your requirements and check whether or not the product matches your criteria.

Once you pick your obvious choices, you can compare them and then select a product that fulfills your criteria. Your online search is going to be a lot more fruitful when you use reputable online mortgage websites. You surely don't want to spend hours finding more about a product based on outdated numbers.

It is better if you select websites that offer the rates from lenders in your area. This turns out to be a more beneficial option because you get to interact with your local lender. There are chances you come across some great local deals which you would have missed otherwise. Besides some special deals, you'll also get a clear picture of all the deals available in your area.

You also have to calculate the fees and other charges you need to pay with the monthly installment. In many cases, the rates displayed on the website don't include the additional cost. That is why it is important to add various costs to the total cost before you sign the deal.

Also, you need to look at mortgage fundamentals before you make a final choice. We'll take a closer look at the fundamentals in the next chapter but for now, let's recall what we've discussed until now.

- *A number of lenders, both in person and online offer mortgages and you can choose one that suits your needs and gives you the best rates.*
- *If you are interested in buying a home, you can also hire a mortgage broker to help you find the best mortgage deal.*
- *Before you decide to sign the deal, make sure you know about the additional costs involved in the process. If a lender offers you a loan with hidden costs, it is not the right deal for you. Continue your search until you find the very best product for yourself.*
- *You'll find plenty of options when searching for a mortgage deal online. If you have the goal of finding the lowest mortgage rates, you should turn to reputable mortgage websites.*

Chapter Six: Mortgage Fundamentals

Different mortgage products are available in the market these days, so making a choice can become really tough. After reading through the next few pages, you'll get to know some of the most important factors you need to consider before signing a mortgage deal.

Fixed and Adjustable Loans

If you choose adjustable rate mortgages, your monthly payments are prone to fluctuation which means the amount of money you have to spend as mortgage payment can change every month.

Choosing an adjustable rate mortgage is a smart choice if you know that interest rates are going to fall. However, if the interest rate goes up, your monthly payments can become significantly higher and you could actually find yourself in hot water!

This is not written to scare you in anyway. You do have other options, and fixed rate mortgage is one of them. If you choose a fixed mortgage product, you won't have to worry about higher monthly payments.

This is because fixed rate mortgages have a **fixed interest rate** you have to pay throughout the term of your loan. This means you can easily calculate how much money you have to pull out from your pocket as mortgage repayment. Fixed rate mortgages are excellent if you want to know how much income you will have left after making the payment every month.

Generally, fixed rate mortgages have a slightly higher interest rate when compared to adjustable rate mortgages. If you choose a fixed rate plan, you will still have to make higher payments even if the interest rates fall. This however, is just one side of the story.

You will be happy with your decision of making fixed payments if the interest rates go up. Regardless of the increase in interest rates, you will make the same payments as you used to earlier.

Some mortgage lenders offer products where you have to pay fixed rates for a specified period and then your plan changes to adjustable rate mortgage when the time period expires.

So if you are not sure whether you can afford to handle rising interest rates, you can go for fixed rate mortgage for, say, ten years and then switch to adjustable rate mortgage.

Remember, the period for which you fix your payments can be extended after agreement with the lender. This is helpful for those who don't feel confident about making higher mortgage payments every month.

Moreover, you can choose to make larger monthly payments with fixed rates and decrease the principal of your loan faster.

With adjustable rate mortgage, you don't really enjoy the same peace of mind that comes with fixed rate mortgage. This is because adjustable rate mortgages or **ARM** have interest rates that change with the changing market conditions.

Changes in interest rates change the size of your monthly mortgage payment, which is one of the main reasons why most borrowers prefer fixed rate mortgages over ARM.

How often does this change happen? Well, interest rates change usually once a year, but there are six month ARMs and two year adjustable rate mortgages. This does not mean adjustable rate mortgages are bad.

ARMs still look attractive to home buyers because initial interest rates are significantly lower if you compare them to what you find with fixed rate mortgages.

Which is Better – Short-term Mortgage or Long-term Loan?

Should I lock-in to a short term mortgage or go for a long term loan? Fixed mortgage deal definitely looks better while interest rates are low, but you have to answer one important question. Which deal is better – short term or long term?

A short term deal gives you more flexibility in terms of planning your budget, whereas long term deals can give more security. In the next few pages, we'll look at the pros and cons of short and long term mortgage plans.

What do you get in a short-term deal?

The most obvious advantage you gain with a short-term deal is the flexibility this short period of time offers. You know exactly how much your payment will be and you can easily make your plans for a couple of years.

Just in case you see that your plan is becoming less competitive, you can switch to other mortgage products that are offering a much better deal. All you have to do is to wait for the term to get over and continue looking for a better deal during that time.

On the other hand, if you have locked in a long term deal, you have to stick to the non competitive deal and wait longer to get rid of it. Breaking the deal is also not a viable option because you have to pay lots of charges as a penalty to end the deal prematurely.

You can say that short term deals are best for you if you don't want to end up in an awkward situation in 5 or 10 years. By fixing yourself only for a couple of years, you give yourself more freedom to evaluate your financial situation, not to mention that mortgage market is very prone to changes.

Are There Any Drawbacks of a Short-Term Deal?

Although short-term deals give you the flexibility of changing your plan, you'll soon find yourself doing lots of work after your term gets over. Moreover, if you decide to extend your fixed period, it would've been better if you had picked up a longer-term deal right at the start.

You also need to remember that you will have to pay application and other related fee when your short term deal ends. Not only does this bring additional hassle, but you might end up paying loads of extra money. If you selected a long term deal, mortgage can be shifted to the back of your mind for several years.

You also have to bear in mind that attractive deals are really difficult to come by, considering the harsh economic climate these days. Because you have to look for a new deal when your short term plan ends, you may find yourself with practically no option in the end. Therefore, if you want to avoid facing such a situation, it would be better if you go for a long term fix.

Are Long-term Fixed Deals More Favorable?

Long-term deals are considered more stable because they lock you in for a longer period of time. You don't have to search for deals every couple of years and you are also protected from abrupt rise in interest rates for the duration you've fixed the deal.

It is quite logical to assume that you can stay safe 'financially' after locking yourself into a long term fix. Generally, long term deals continue for 5, 10 or 25 years. Because your interest rate will not change during that time, your finances become more reliable.

Another distinct advantage of long term deal is that you have greater control over your budget.

All you have to do is make a note of what you have to pay every month at the beginning of your term and then forget about revising your monthly payment until your term ends.

Since mortgage payments are one of the most sensitive expenditures, sparing yourself from the hassle of searching for a new competitive deal could really benefit you.

Not to mention, you'll also save lots of money because you don't have to pay new application fee as you would normally do if you had a short-term fix.

Are There Any Drawbacks of a Long-Term Deal?

The interest rates you get on a long term deal tend to be slightly higher than what you get on short term deals. This means there's a possibility that you pay more in a long term deal. However, another factor that makes people reluctant to choose long term deals is the unpredictability of interest rates in the future.

You can only guess whether the rates will go up, get lowered or stay the same right till the end of your term. So, if you lock in a deal for long term basis, you'll miss out on attractive deals, if interest rates fall over the next few years.

Of course, you will be happy with a low rate, long term deal if the interest rates go up, but if the rates drop further, your long term deal can become uncompetitive.

What's even more unfortunate is the fact that you cannot switch your deal before your term ends. Actually, long term deals have no easy way out because there are a number of penalties and extra charges if you want to get rid of your agreement before term. Even if you find yourself stuck in a deal that's expensive, you still cannot do anything about it.

Remember, you have to make a decision about a short term or long term deal after considering your personal circumstances. Go for a deal which benefits you and your finances. And it is always a good idea to get some advice from a reputable mortgage broker or a mortgage expert before going ahead with a decision.

Fine-tuning Your Selection

You are now familiar with the strengths and weaknesses of short term and long term deals, so it is time to assess your selection of loans. “Which loan is best for you” is a difficult question to answer but here’s how you can find a suitable answer to your question.

- Take a look at a direction in which interest rates are heading. Interest rates can go up, down or stay the same.
- How much payment can you easily afford?
- How long do you intend to live in your new home?
- Can you easily handle the hassles of adjustable rate mortgages if the interest rates change?

You can select adjustable rate mortgages if:

- You only want to concentrate on making low payments for a long time.
- You expect interest rates to fall and don’t want to search for a new deal.

On the other hand, fixed rate mortgages are the way to go if:

- You prefer making predictable payment in the near future.
- You sense that interest rates can climb over the next few years.

Your decision is also largely dependent on your personal circumstances. Whether or not you want a new home is largely your choice, but you also have to see whether or not you can afford the monthly mortgage payments.

In addition to loan features or lender's criteria, it is better if you take a look at some factors of your own.

Your Gross Monthly Income

Ask yourself a few questions.

- Will you be able to rely on your income to pay for the plan you've selected?
- Have you made the right choice considering your wages?
- Is your monthly income enough to make the mortgage payment and fulfill your other expenses?
- Do you have a plan just in case you lose your current job?

Your Monthly and Future Expenses

Your lender wants to have a look at your current monthly expenses when calculating the back-end ratio, but have you thought about other expenses that you have to manage while making mortgage payments?

Remember, your selection may vary if your kids will go to college in the future or your family has plans to buy a new car. You also have to rethink your choice if you enjoy going for vacations every year.

Your Financial Habits

Are you willing to improve your savings or change your spending habits? Will you stick to the same old habits after getting a mortgage? Often getting approved for a mortgage means that you have to tighten your budget or cut down your expenses.

If you cannot make the compromises that are needed, maybe this is not the right time to go for a deal. You might do better if you play safe and apply for a loan only when you are mentally prepared for it.

Interestingly, you also have to consider your own personality in addition to your financial habits.

Some people can stay cool even if they have to pay more than $4000 every month for, let's say, the next 15 or 30 years. If you can sleep peacefully knowing that you have to cut down your expenses to make your mortgage payment, you are more likely to be happy about your purchase.

Your Troubles Don't End After Getting Approved

Buying a new home definitely looks exciting, but there are factors that are more important than simply getting approved for a loan. For example, some expenses associated with homes just don't go even after you finish paying your mortgage payments. Smart homeowners always keep the following things in mind.

Maintenance Costs

If you buy a new home, the expensive appliances and accessories you put inside are not going to stay new forever. Don't assume that after you get through your mortgage schedule, you won't have to spend more money. You could find yourself in a bad situation if you have to finance major repairs in your new home.

You also cannot ignore spending on *furniture and décor* of your new home. You definitely want to have a few magnificent interior lights to lighten your empty room. The same applies to curtains and furniture that need to be placed in every room. So before you buy a new home, make sure you have enough finances to cover the decorating costs of your latest buy.

Your Utility Bills

Your finances are going to take a setback if you don't include electricity, water, trash removal, cable television, telephone and gas charges in your list of expenses when applying for a mortgage. Remember, these expenses cannot be avoided if you really want to become a proud homeowner.

Some planned communities ask homeowners to pay monthly or yearly association fees for lawn maintenance, snow removal or other community services. Sometimes this fee may cover the costs of maintaining home exterior. You may have to pay less than $100 or several hundred dollars per month depending on the community you select.

It is better if you assess the costs before buying your home and find out what your association fee will cover. Here's a friendly advice: Remember that like any other expense, association fee is also likely to increase over time.

Evaluate Your Financial Risk

The cost of your new home is the single largest personal expense you will ever face. So before you take on such an enormous debt, it is better if you take out some time to do some math.

When you sit down to evaluate your financial risk, consider your present personal situation, and think about your future. Making an informed decision at this stage will make sure that you don't have to compromise your future.

Mortgages and Interest Rates

To put it simply, you have to pay lower interest rates on your loan when you have a high credit score. If you have a look at the table below, you can see that borrowers having a credit score of 760 to 850 have to pay a 3.55% interest rate on their 30 year fixed rate mortgage.

Note: **All figures shown in the table below are given for illustrative purposes only.** It is assumed that borrowers have a principal amount of

$100,000. All values are based on National Averages.

Credit Score	Interest Rate
760-850	3.55%
700-759	3.772%
660-679	4.163%
640-659	4.593%
620-639	5.139%

You are familiar with mortgage fundamentals and it's time to recall what we've discussed in the previous pages.

- *The ideal mortgage plan you choose can be fixed rate or adjustable rate. If you go for a fix rate deal, your interest rate remains the same throughout the term of your mortgage. On the other hand, if you go for an adjustable rate loan, your monthly mortgage payments will change depending on the changes in interest rates.*

- *You also have a choice to go for a short-term deal or opt for a long-term deal. Remember, each has its own set of pros and cons. Short-term deals look better because you get a chance to sign a different deal just in case your existing deal becomes unattractive. Moreover, you can change your plan immediately after your existing deal expires.*

- *Long-term deals seem to be a wiser option if you want to put monthly mortgage payments at the back of your mind for a long time. However, you need to remember that breaking a long-term deal is never easy. You'll have to pay lots of money as penalty if you decide to back out of your agreement before your term ends.*

- *Before you finalize a mortgage deal, you'll have to consider additional factors such as existing trend in interest rate, your gross monthly income, financial habit, future expenses, maintenance costs and utility bills. Remember, your task does not get over once your mortgage is paid off. Buying a home means that there are lots of extra expenses that need to be managed for the rest of your life.*

- *It is better if you evaluate your personal risk before making a final decision.*

- *Recall that your lender will look at your credit history to decide the interest you have to pay. Your mortgage interest terms are likely to be more favorable when you have the highest credit score possible.*

Chapter Seven: Comparing Your Mortgage Choices

You know that you will need a mortgage when you are going to buy a home. But, you just cannot walk up to any lender and ask for a mortgage. It is obvious that you will shop around, do your homework and then select a deal that benefits you in the long run.

Beware of Internet Pirates

A number of mortgage deals can also be found online and you need to feel secure before you finalize your deal and select a lender. Here's how you can make the most when you apply for a mortgage product online.

1. Gather and scrutinize your personal and credit information before you start filling in an online application.

2. Consider applying on websites that are reliable and guarantee security of information. Remember, there are a large number of "internet pirates" that offer loans on false terms.

   Sometimes, online products may ask you to make additional payment in the form of a third party or closing costs. You must watch out and stay away from every product that does not give you the clear details. In short, you must work with an online lender that gives you a complete listing of all fees and charges.

3. If you enjoy perusing the online mortgage websites, you would be pleased with the interactive features offered by online brokers

and lenders. You can compare the total cost of your loan considering different factors including the time period for which you'll keep the loan and what will happen to the interest rate during the same period.

4. By using the online comparison feature, you have the best chance of finding a good deal in your area. All you have to do is enter your desired price, amount of down payment and the desirable location. The website will then display the best results based on your search criteria.

5. It is better if you take a look at loan features before you lock your lender.

Take a Look at Loan Features

- Comparing loans from different lenders is one of the most difficult parts of mortgage shopping.
- In addition to interest rate, you have to keep a close eye on quoted rate, points and closing costs.
- Closing costs in mortgages typically include related fee, title charges, escrow charges and transfer charges.
- You also have to pay close attention to maximum LTV, insurance payments if any, credit requirements, prepayment penalty and conversion options.
- Make sure you don't overstretch yourself. Doing so can harm you in the long run. Go for

the deal that offers you a decent sized loan you can easily repay.

- There are so many different lenders in the market and they all offer different products. Once you have more than one option, you can review the interest rates, closing costs and the length of loan period.
- You have the best chance of landing at the best place when you shop for loans all over.
- Don't neglect online lenders and banks when you check for the deals that suit your plan.
- You also need to remember the following information.
- Mortgage principal amount. You can find this number by subtracting down payment from the price of your home.
- Mortgage term. This will be the length of term your loan will last.

- Interest rate. Once you have a projected interest rate, you will know how much you have to pay every month.

Tips for a Good Borrowing Experience

If you are new and don't know much about the concept of mortgages, here is something you need to know about the market. Like any other investment, it is important that you get the mortgage basics absolutely right.

The following list gives you the main points you need to bear in mind when looking for mortgage products.

1. Shop around wisely, not a surprising tip you would say. After all, you know that all things can be deceiving at first glance. The point is, don't jump into the first deal that is offered to you. This may save you time, but remember,

you will be quite pleased if you take out time and search the market for the best deal.

2. Not all lenders offer a good rate; but if you've got a good credit score, there are chances you find a plan that has lower monthly payments.

3. It is better if you research your local market and catch up with the latest news in your region. You can even ask someone who has recently bought a home about their experience with a particular lender and make a more informed decision.

4. Understand the costs and fees commonly associated with a mortgage. As mentioned earlier, you can find the costs sorted out in the glossary section.

   And, remember you might be asked to pay additional costs depending on factors like type of mortgage, the amount of loan, the lender you select and last, your state.

5. In case, you haven't thought about this earlier, lenders actually want you to be quite honest about your financial standing when you decide to borrow money.

   There is no reason you should give false information to cover any imperfections you have on your financial record. Remember, you can still find a suitable deal when you are honest about your financial standing.

   On a separate note, even lenders and brokers these days are more careful about whom they select for a loan.

   There is a lot more paperwork involved, details of which can be found in the later chapters. In short, be clear about what you say to your lender because your lender will definitely verify every bit of information you submit.

6. We have discussed a lot about it, but your credit score is the number one thing that can ensure a good borrowing experience. Keep in mind that your FICO score is not just a number, because it has a big say in the interest rate you get for your product.

   If you want to get the best deals, you'll need to maintain a credit score of 720 or higher. And you know that higher the score, the better is the deal you get from your lender.

7. Well, this tip may be easier said than done. You can make a big down payment and impress your lender right at the start. Remember, this will be a real biggie and your lender will be very keen to give you the loan.

Are You Paying a Fair Price for Your Loan?

Buying a home is a major purchase and most buyers don't have enough cash on hand. Luckily mortgage provides you with the capital required to become a proud home owner, but the question is "are you paying a fair price for your loan?"

Actually, you have to repay the loan along with interest and you need to find out whether the deal is affordable or not.

For example:

You have $25,000 in cash and want to buy a home that is listed for $200,000. How do you proceed? You can make a down payment of $25,000, which leaves you with a mortgage principal of $175,000.

From the different choices you have, let's assume that you select a product that offers you a 25 year mortgage at a fixed rate of 6%. This means you have to pull out $1,127.53 as monthly mortgage payment.

After making this monthly payment over the period of 25 years, you will become the proud owner of your home. However, not only you have to repay the original mortgage principal, i.e. $175,000, but you have to pay an additional $163,000 in interest over the entire term.

This means your home that was originally priced at $200,000, really costs more than $360,000! You can save money by making a little ‘extra’ payment every month to get rid of the loan faster. To be exact, you can save thousands by paying off your loan faster.

Let’s say you repay your loan in 15 years, this will cut down the total amount of interest you pay by $73,000. Remember, mortgages help you buy a home, but a little understanding of how monthly payments work can help you save lots of money in the long run. After all, mortgages too are a type of debt; and the faster you get rid of it, the more money you can save by paying less as interest.

How Much Down Payment is Needed?

You might be asked to put down a cash payment of 5%, 10% or 20% of the total sale price of your home depending on the lender. Interestingly, if you put down more cash than what your lender asks, let's say 25% or 30%, you can be quite lucky as your lender might be willing to overlook the minor blemishes in your credit report and approve your loan application.

Just in case you don't have enough cash for down payment or you can only pay less than 20% of the total buying price of your home, you may be asked to obtain **private mortgage insurance**

(PMI). This will act as a protection for your lender when your loan gets approved.

Remember, you can lower your monthly mortgage payment or afford a more luxurious home when you put more money down as down payment.

What did we discuss in this chapter?

- *You can find the best mortgage deals online, but you need to shop around before making a final decision. Make sure that you are dealing with reputable websites so that your finances and personal information remains secure.*

- *You must take a close look at the loan features such as closing costs, interest rates and term of mortgage if you want to improve your chances of becoming a successful homeowner.*

- *You also need to know how your credit score is considered by lenders in addition to other factors that can affect your borrowing experience. As mentioned earlier, you need to shop around for the best deal as it can help you get a mortgage plan you can easily afford.*

- *Knowing how much you have to pay as monthly mortgage payment over the term can help you determine whether or not you are paying a fair price for your loan. Remember you can save thousands of dollars by getting rid of your mortgage faster.*

- *Generally, the amount of down payment you have to put down becomes one of the biggest obstacles to proud homeownership. Fortunately, you can also find lenders that are willing to approve your application even with small down payments.*

Chapter Eight: Moving Ahead – Mortgage Paperwork

Buying a home requires paperwork on both the lender's side and your side. Moreover, there is lots of paperwork involved as you have to give a few things to the lender and there are some documents the lender must give you. But you don't have to worry. Mortgage documentation does seem overwhelming, but you'll find a very good general idea of what you are going to need.

In this particular chapter, we'll look at some of the most obvious paperwork you'll have to make before you can move ahead with the transaction. It is better if you get familiar with the documents you need to provide as stated by the law. First of all, congratulate yourself because you are moving closer to your ultimate goal, i.e. buying your dream home.

Here's a friendly reminder for those of you who are suspecting lots of work. Before you talk to a mortgage lender, pull out a copy of your credit report and examine it carefully. You must also check your report before you begin shopping.

If you find that you have a low FICO score, you are more likely to benefit from an **FHA loan**. These loans don't consider your FICO score and you can make down payments as low as 2.85%.

Do inform your employer before you start processing your loan application. Your lender will most probably contact your employer for verification of information you have provided. In addition you have to provide the following documents.

The Documents Checklist

Keep the following documents in one place just in case your lender asks for them.

Here are some additional tips for how you should gather your documents.

- Some lenders want bank statements and pay stubs for two months while others can ask you to submit three months of records. You can make a copy of each statement but don't hand out the original.

- Similarly if you own mutual funds, stocks or bonds, you can make a copy of each and show it on demand.

- Make sure the tax returns you submit to the lender are signed by you.

- Most lenders prefer hard copies of asset records, but you can also show online statements if that's how you receive your records and statements.

- If you decide to meet the lender in person, you can bring your driver's license to identify yourself.

- It is better if you bring your Home Sales Contract with the purchase price mentioned along with you just in case you've found the home you want to buy.

- Even though it is needless to mention, make sure your documents are complete and correct. Never submit incomplete or false documents with an assumption that your lender will "fill in" or "fix" your records later.

Remember, not all lenders require the same documentation and if you have really strong credit scores, you might have to provide very little of it. But you can always save your time and energy by carrying all the documents during the application process.

Filling Out the Loan Application

Now that you've read about the key documents in the mortgage application process, it is time to take a closer look at the application form. There are a number of important steps involved in your mortgage loan application and the official form is known as ***Uniform Residential Loan Application***.

The application form consists of several sections and you'll know what you have to provide under each section after reading through the next few pages. You can also hire a reputable loan officer to fill in your application correctly.

Remember, you can seriously damage your reputation if you put false information on your mortgage application. Every bit of information entered on the application form remains confidential and is protected by federal laws.

If you look over the mortgage application form closely, you'll see that there are 10 sections.

Section 1: Type of Mortgage and Terms of Loan

Here, you have to mention the type of loan and mortgage terms. If you haven't selected your dream property, you can enter the specific amount of money you intend to borrow.

Section 2: Purpose of Loan and Property Information

This section deals with information about your property including the address and other details. You will also have to describe the purpose you are applying for a loan.

Section 3: Borrower's Information

As the name suggests you have to provide your personal information, such as your name, Social

Security number, date of birth and contact details. Moreover, you also have to provide information about the additional borrower if applicable. This applies if your spouse accepts the responsibility of paying the mortgage amount with you.

Section 4: Employment Information

You have to provide the details of your employment. If you haven't worked at your current position for at least two years, you will have to provide details about your previous job until you have a two year record. You also need to provide federal W-2 income tax forms for the last two years.

In addition, you will be asked to sign a VOE (Verification of Employment) form which will be sent to your employer to verify your current job position and earnings.

Section 5: Monthly Income and Housing Expense Information

Filling out this section is important to know how much money you will have after taking out taxes and other expenses. Putting it simply, you have to include all sources of income that you will consider to repay your loan.

Section 6: Assets and Liabilities

This section basically defines your "Net Worth". If you want to know how much you're worth, all you have to do is subtract the amount you owe (liability) from the amount you own (i.e. your assets).

You can mention your investments, bank accounts, savings, stocks and bonds under the asset section. For the liability section, you'll have to list your credit card bills, auto loans and all other monthly expenses.

Section 7: Details of Transaction

This perhaps is the most important section of your report where you have to give the purchase price of your home and the total cost of mortgage including principal, interest rate, lender fee and closing costs.

Section 8: Declarations

You will be asked questions related to current or past legal problems that can have an influence on your financial standing. This includes bankruptcy declaration or your status of citizenship in the United States.

Section 9: Acknowledgement and Agreement

You have to sign your name saying that the information you've provided is true to the best of your knowledge.

Section 10: Information for Government Purposes

In the last section of your application, you have to provide information such as your ethnic origin and race. This information is used for government monitoring.

Signing the Agreement

Once your application form is complete and duly filled, you will be asked to sign it so that it is sent for approval. Your chances of getting approved for a mortgage are really bright if you have a preapproval letter.

Since you have provided important documents and information to the lender under federal laws, your lender must also provide a **Good Faith Estimate** and summary of your costs within three days of applying for a loan.

The Good Faith Estimate provides you with an estimate of your mortgage terms. If you are approved for a loan, you can use the information presented in the Good Faith Estimate to evaluate your terms before accepting it.

Basically GFE is a three page form with summary on the first page, your settlement charges on the second page and optional tables on the last page.

- **Summary of Your Loan**

This section describes the basic terms of your loan including principal amount, loan term, your interest rate and monthly mortgage payment. You are also given additional information about prepayment penalty and changes in interest rate (if applicable).

- **Settlement Charges**

These include fees charged by your lender for submitting your loan application in addition to origination charges. Other settlement charges include appraisal fee and cost of credit report.

You have to understand that Good Faith Estimate is only an estimate and actual charges may differ. Moreover, you also need to have a clear idea of how much you are paying and why.

Chapter Nine: Refinancing Your Mortgage

Mortgages often are the longest term debt to repay since average home loans last for 15, 25 or 30 years. Your home is your biggest investment and that's one of the major reasons why smart homeowners are looking for ways to minimize their debt and maximize their **equity** at the same time.

Refinancing simply means that you get a new mortgage with a goal to reduce your old monthly payments, lower your interest rate or make other purchases such as cars.

Some of the obvious reasons homeowners go for refinancing include:

1. Get lower interest rates.

When you apply for a loan at lower interest rate, you can save lots of money on your monthly mortgage payments.

In short, you can swap a higher interest mortgage with the new deal to increase your savings.

2. Switch your mortgage product.

You can go for refinancing if you want to get rid of your adjustable rate loan because the interest rates are going to rise.

If you switch to fixed rate mortgage, you no longer have to deal with changing interest rates and your payments will become consistent.

3. Refinance and Home Equity

Refinancing from a 30 year fixed rate loan to a 15 year fixed rate loan can greatly reduce your long-term interest charges and you can pay off your debt quickly.

Want to Avoid the Worst Refinance?

Before you contact a lender for refinance, ask yourself a few questions. If you are able to answer these questions successfully, you'll know that whether or not refinancing makes sense for you.

1. How long will you stay in your home? If you don't plan to stay for the next five years, refinancing is not the choice for you.

2. Does your loan have a prepayment penalty? Ask your lender whether or not you have to pay a penalty for paying off your debt faster.

   If you have to pay an extra amount as legal costs, refinancing may not be right for you.

3. Will your savings be increased? Needless to say, you will have to pay some charges for taking out an extra loan.

So before you claim a refinance, you have to see whether your overall savings will be increased during the process or not.

4. Are interest rates going to climb? You can consider refinancing from an ARM to fixed rate mortgage if the interest rates are going to rise.

Keep a Close Eye on Your Numbers

Refinance does help homeowners a great deal, but you need to do your math right and understand how the new loan will affect you. Here are some numbers that can influence your mortgage refinance rate.

Know How You Can Restructure Finances

If you have troubles making payment on your mortgage loan, you can adjust the terms of loans with a little help from financial restructuring.

Restructuring your loan can help you accommodate mortgage monthly payments in your budget and save money.

You have to approach your lender in case you want to modify your mortgage terms. When your lender agrees to the modified plan, you will be required to pay the remaining amount of money over a longer or shorter period of time. However, there are a few things you need to keep in mind.

- Restructuring your loan can cause interest rates to change and your lender may charge you more to compensate for extra time allotted.
- Like every other legal contract, both you and your lender have to agree to the revised terms of mortgage. Most homeowners prefer to refinance their mortgage because their current lender will not be involved in the process.

Is Refinancing a Good Move?

Like every homeowner you will be frightened about losing your dream home. Refinancing does have its own set of advantages but it really doesn't work if you've had your mortgage for a very long time.

Similarly, it is also not a good move if you have a prepayment penalty on your mortgage deal or you've decided to move to another place in less than five years.

On the other hand, refinancing is a good move if you want to change from an ARM to a fixed rate deal. Often refinancing becomes a useful option when you have to get your interest rate lowered.

Chapter Ten: Must-Knows About Mortgages

Top Mortgage Mistakes You Need to Avoid

After reading through the initial chapters, you know that getting a mortgage is no simple task. You can say that it is one of the most complex transactions of your life, at least in terms of money. Here are some common pitfalls you need to avoid to get the most of your mortgage plan.

1. Don't neglect your credit report. Before you apply for mortgage, take out time to evaluate your creditworthiness. Remember, having a bad credit score can leave you with practically "no mortgage options."

2. Never apply for any type of new credit before and during the process of applying for a

mortgage. This is because new credit inquiries can drain your credit score and your application can be rejected. And, if you are lucky enough to be approved, you have to handle higher interest rates, which definitely is not a good experience for any borrower.

3. If you are applying for a home loan, you need to add your property taxes, insurance premiums and housing costs to your overall mortgage amount. Failing to look at the additional payments can actually leave your savings in bad shape right at the start.

4. You may be convinced about your assets, but your lender also needs to be convinced that you can actually repay your loan. Make sure you have enough assets and savings to show at the time you apply for a loan.

5. Since you have decided to apply for a mortgage, you also have to stick to your current employment. Remember, hopping around in search of better jobs at the time of loan application can lead to problems.

6. Do spend some time to get preapproved for the loan. Remember, borrowers who are preapproved look more attractive to a lender. This is because lenders know that they can afford the loan.

7. As mentioned earlier, the worst mistake you can do is jumping into the first deal you come across. Comparing choices can actually give you more options when it comes to making a final choice.

8. Always deal with reputable dealers and go for a loan program you clearly understand. Remember, going to exotic programs that are

too good to be true can cost you dearly in the long run.

9. You will be happier with your deal if you decide to lock your mortgage rate.

10. Last, make sure you read every word of your loan agreement to avoid signing up for something you don't agree on.

Understand Bankruptcy and Foreclosure

Foreclosure is a process in which your home becomes a property of the lending institution, i.e. your lender. You can get into this situation if you are late on your home payments and pay absolutely no attention to the warning letters issued by your lender. Remember, this behavior can cost you dearly as you will be standing in midst of a tough financial situation.

If you feel that you cannot make your monthly mortgage payments or your payments will get delayed, waste no time and request your lender to extend the date. You can actually save your home from foreclosure if you maintain a good credit reputation.

Similarly, if you have declared bankruptcy in the past, you'll know that it is difficult to get approved for a home loan. However, you can improve your chances by rebuilding your credit history. The fact is that you can get approved for a home loan if your credit report shows promising progress and you are really serious about improving your habits.

Turning Denied Loans into Approved Loans

One of the biggest reasons your mortgage application gets denied is that your lenders are not really convinced about your creditworthiness. Often blemishes on your credit report, low FICO scores, lack of savings or unstable employment record work against you and your loan does not get approved.

You shouldn't be worried after reading all this because you still have a chance of turning your denied loan application into approved loan. All you have to do is change your financial habits and start rebuilding your credit history. You will actually be quite pleased with your hard work when your credit score improves and your lender is willing to grant you a loan.

Closing Your Loan in the Best Way

Once your loan application gets approved, the only thing left is your loan closing. Usually loan closing takes place at an escrow office and you are likely to find:

- An Escrow officer
- A Closing agent
- Yourself and any other co-borrower
- Your real estate agent
- Your seller's real estate agent at the loan closing.

The closing process isn't complicated and here's a brief description of what will happen.

- You have to first sign a document that you have accepted a mortgage from your lender.
- Your lender will then transfer the money to the seller and this will transfer the ownership rights of property to you.
- Additionally there will be several declarations and documents you have to sign. To keep things simple, remember that these

documents show your financial obligations and that you have to repay your loan.

It is important that you read all the documents carefully before you sign them and don't ever hesitate to ask questions. The day you close your loan will surely be one of the most memorable days of your life because you have a home to enjoy in the future.

Chapter Eleven: See Whether Your Loan Has Paid You Well!

At the end of this eBook, you will be aware of every detail of the complex process that is known as mortgage application. We all know that life is unpredictable and signing of the mortgage document is only the start of your responsibilities as a homeowner.

If you want to prepare for the future, you need to continue with your good financial habits. So best of luck for your future and hope that you stick with your goal of organizing finances so that you can comfortably stay in your dream home. This has been a great journey so far and here's hoping that we meet again very soon.

Glossary

The following terms have been used in this eBook and relate to the mortgage application process.

Adjustable-Rate Mortgage (ARM):

ARM is a type of mortgage plan where your monthly payments can change when interest rate changes.

Annual Percentage Rate (APR):

APR basically tells you how much your loan will cost annually. This includes your interest rate, broker fee and other charges you are required to pay as a borrower.

Collateral:

The property which will be used as security for a loan or debt. When you apply for mortgage, your home will act as the collateral.

Closing Costs:

The costs you have to pay to complete the mortgage transaction process. These costs are in addition to the amount you'll pay as the price of your home.

Down Payment:

It is a portion of the total price of your home and is usually paid upfront. Down payment is not considered a part of your mortgage principal amount.

Escrow:

It is the deposit you have to make to the lender to pay property taxes, insurance premiums, and other expenses.

Equity:

The value of your home above the total mortgage amount you owe for your home.

Fixed-Rate Mortgage:

A mortgage deal where your interest rate does not change throughout the term of your loan.

Lock-In Rate:

It is a written agreement from your lender showing that you'll pay a specific mortgage interest rate for a specific amount of time.

Mortgage Rate:

The interest rate you have to pay when you borrow money to buy a home.

Principal:

The amount of money you borrow from the lender to buy your home.

Made in the USA
Monee, IL
04 November 2026

67384917R00098